❧ *Praise for* THE RAVEN AND THE DOVE, ❧
THE BIG FISH, *and*
THE STUBBORN DONKEY

"Sandy Eisenberg Sasso has a gift for sparking religious imagination in children — and in the rest of us. In her new book, three iconic biblical stories are told from the animals' perspectives and new life and meaning is breathed into them. The unwilling raven, the whale who describes Jonah as a 'bitter pill,' and the donkey who knows herself to be her master's 'greatest asset' are a delight. Fresh, funny, and wise, this book is a treat."

— **Jennifer Grant**, author of *Maybe God Is Like That Too* and *A Little Blue Bottle*

"A donkey who would appreciate it if her owner, Balaam, thanked her once in a while. A giant fish who complains that swallowing Jonah gave him indigestion. Combine this with a clever collaboration between a raven and dove on Noah's ark and you have a delightful reimagining of biblical tales from animal perspectives. Sandy Eisenberg Sasso writes with verve and insight, giving readers much to enjoy."

— **Jacqueline Jules**, author of *The Generous Fish* and *Never Say a Mean Word Again*

"In these wise and witty tales, animals invite us to look through their eyes for a fresh view of some familiar stories. A big-hearted whale, a perceptive donkey, and the pragmatic partnership of raven and dove teach us about new life, compassion, and the true nature of blessing. Through her playful yet respectful handling of biblical texts, Sasso reminds us that God speaks in surprising ways, and that we still have much to learn from other creatures. Perfect for reading aloud, this collection is sure to spark laughter and deep wondering among adults and children alike."

— **Laura Alary**, author of *Breathe: A Child's Guide to Ascension, Pentecost, and the Growing Time* and *Read, Wonder, Listen: Stories from the Bible for Young Readers*

THE RAVEN AND THE DOVE, THE BIG FISH, *and* THE STUBBORN DONKEY

Stories of Animals from the Bible

S<small>ANDY</small> E<small>ISENBERG</small> S<small>ASSO</small>

I<small>LLUSTRATED BY</small> R<small>OY</small> D<small>E</small>L<small>EON</small>

PARACLETE PRESS
BREWSTER, MASSACHUSETTS

2021 First Printing

The Raven and the Dove, The Big Fish, and The Stubborn Donkey:
Stories of Animals from the Bible

ISBN 978-1-64060-663-0

Quotations from the Bible are taken from the Jewish Publication Society TANAKH
translation copyright © 1985 by the Jewish Publication Society

The Paraclete Press name and logo (dove on cross) are trademarks of Paraclete Press

   Library of Congress Cataloging-in-Publication Data
Names: Sasso, Sandy Eisenberg, author. | DeLeon, Roy, illustrator.
Title: The raven and the dove, the big fish, and the stubborn donkey :
   stories of animals from the Bible / Sandy Eisenberg Sasso ; illustrated
   by Roy DeLeon.
Description: Brewster, Massachusetts : Paraclete Press, 2021. | Audience:
   Ages 10 | Audience: Grades 4-6 | Summary: "In this charmingly
   illustrated book, animals of the Bible tell their own story, teaching us
   the value of all living beings, and something about ourselves"--
   Provided by publisher.
Identifiers: LCCN 2021025970 (print) | LCCN 2021025971 (ebook) | ISBN
   9781640606630 | ISBN 9781640606647 (epub) | ISBN 9781640606654 (pdf)
Subjects: LCSH: Bible stories, English. | BISAC: JUVENILE NONFICTION /
   Religion / Bible Stories / Old Testament | RELIGION / Christian
   Education / Children & Youth
Classification: LCC BS551.3 .S27 2021 (print) | LCC BS551.3 (ebook) | DDC
   220.95/05--dc23
LC record available at https://lccn.loc.gov/2021025970
LC ebook record available at https://lccn.loc.gov/2021025971

10 9 8 7 6 5 4 3 2 1

Published by Paraclete Press
Brewster, Massachusetts
www.paracletepress.com

Printed in the United States of America

For Darwin, Ari, Levi, and Raven,
who taught me a love of animals.

—SANDY

May all beings and creatures living on Mother Earth
be in harmony with the will of the Creator.

—ROY

CONTENTS

———

AUTHOR'S INTRODUCTION

Animals appear throughout the Bible from the very beginning. On the fifth day of creation, "God said, 'Let the waters bring forth swarms of living creatures and birds that fly above the earth across the expanse of the sky. God created the great sea monsters, and all the living creatures of every kind that creep, which the waters brought forth in swarms, and all the winged birds of every kind. And God saw that this was good'" (Genesis 1:20–21).

In the book of Psalms, God proclaims an intimate knowledge of all who creep, fly, and walk on all fours: "For Mine is every animal of the forest, the beasts on a thousand mountains. I know every bird in the mountains; the creatures of the field are subject to me" (Psalm 50:10–11).

From the snake in the Garden of Eden to the lost sheep in Luke's parable, stories about fish and birds, rams and goats abound. They swim and fly, slither and climb all through the pages. The wolf lies down with the lamb, the ram arrives in the knick of time, and foxes run through vineyards. We read about them, but they have no voice of their own.

We hear about these creatures through the words of man and woman. What if we were to allow the animals to speak, to tell us their feelings and their perspective about the world around them and the humans they encounter? What would we learn?

The book of Job says:

"But ask the beasts, and they will teach you;
The birds of the sky, they will tell you,
Or speak to the earth, it will teach you;
The fish of the sea, they will inform you"
(Job 12:7–8).

In the following three stories, we allow the raven and the dove on Noah's ark, the big fish that swallows Jonah, and the donkey on which Balaam rode, to be the narrators of their own stories, to inform us and teach us.

By following the flight of the bird, the way of the big fish through the water, and the trot of the donkey, we re-imagine our stories. We learn something about the intrinsic value of all living beings, and something about ourselves.

THE RAVEN
AND THE DOVE

I am not going!" cawed the raven. "It is noisy and crowded in this ark, but I will not be the first one out. No way!"

"But someone has to go first," insisted Noah. "We can't stay inside this boat forever. We are running out of food. And the smell . . .!"

Noah held his nose.

"Why send me?" croaked Raven. "I haven't caused any trouble. Who knows what it's like outside the ark?"

He pointed with his curved beak to the endless water with no place to rest.

Noah wouldn't budge.

Raven wouldn't fly.

The animals wouldn't stop complaining.

Naamah, Noah's wife, shook her head.

"No way this is this going to work," Naamah said. "The animals are arguing, and so are we. It's a zoo in here! We cannot continue this way for much longer."

Just like Noah, she held her nose from the smell. "Phew!"

She suggested other animals for the task.

Jaguar could run, and Ant could crawl.

Rabbit could hop, and Snake could slither.

Kangaroo could jump, and Monkey could climb.

But with only water as far as they could see, none of them wanted to help.

Naamah decided to talk to Dove. Dove's cooing put her to sleep at night. It wasn't easy. When the lions weren't roaring and the bees buzzing, the chickens were clucking and the rhinoceroses were bellowing. Just when she thought there might be some quiet, the peacocks screamed and the geese cackled.

If Dove's song could give her some peace, maybe Dove would have an idea.

"We can't stay here in the Ark much longer, but everyone is afraid to leave," Naamah said to her feathered friend. "Noah has asked Raven to see if there is land, but he won't go. Maybe he is afraid that he will get lost."

Dove cooed, "I can help. I have a great sense of direction. I will talk to him, bird to bird."

Naamah tried to smile, but she was still shaking.

Dove flew to Raven's nest.

"Let's get away from the other animals," cooed Dove.

Raven hopped to the edge of the Ark and looked out over the expanse of water and shivered.

Dove's head bopped up and down as she began to try and soothe Raven's ruffled feathers.

"We are birds of a feather," she said. "If we can't work this out, nobody can."

"You want to get rid of me too?" Raven screamed.

"Noah hates me because I am too loud, and I sometimes copy the way he talks," Raven said.

"No," Dove insisted. "He does not hate you. Right now, he can't stand any of us. He is tired of the noise and the smell. He is tired of feeding us day and night. He wants out of this ark."

"So, let *him* go," suggested Raven. "Or *you* go, if you think it is such a good idea."

Dove whistled, "I eat fruits and vegetables. The flood has washed them all away. But you eat meat, and you might find food."

Raven was about to say, *Let's wait for God to tell us when it is safe to leave. After all, God told us when to enter.* But on second thought, maybe God was waiting for *him* to do something.

"Remember," cried Raven, "God said, 'Bring two of every kind on the ark.' If I get lost, what will happen to my partner? Without me, she will be all alone in our nest. Without me, there will be no more ravens in the skies —not now, not ever."

"I think I can help," offered Dove. "I always find my way home. If you go, I will keep watch. If you are lost, I will come find you."

Raven did not croak or scream. He did the amazing thing that ravens do: he copied the human voice. He sounded just like Naamah when he told Dove, "You are like a compass. You know north from south, east from west. You know where home is."

Dove responded, "And you are clever. You can caw and warble and do funny tricks. You can even talk like Noah and Naamah."

"Yes," he sighed, "that gets me into lots of trouble." But someone had to do something, and Raven finally agreed he would be the one. "I will go. But you must do two things. Bring me a seed from one of the plants on the ark. And if I do not find land, promise that you will come find me."

Dove agreed. She brought Raven a small green olive seed. She cooed, "Take this and fly free. Drop it so that it can become a tree. I will tell Naamah of our plan."

Raven put the seed in his mouth and flew from the Ark. He went back and forth, back and forth looking for a dry place to stand. Seeing none, he dropped the seed, hoping it would find enough earth to grow roots.

Noah sighed, disappointed that Raven did not sight land. "How long will it take before we can leave this Ark? Enough already!" He shouted into the damp air. Then he buried his face in his hands.

When the days dragged on, Naamah whispered to Noah, "It is time to send Dove."

Noah did not often listen to what others told him. But he had no other ideas. So, Noah sent Dove.

Dove searched for Raven as she had said she would, and kept a lookout for an olive tree. She found Raven, but no tree.

"What happened?" Dove asked Raven. "Water is everywhere. There is no tree. Did you drop the seed I gave you?"

"Be patient," squawked Raven. "A seed takes a long time to grow."

So Dove returned to the Ark. She waited for a while before she flew over the waters a second time.

She flew and she looked. She looked and she flew. Her wings fluttered until they ached. Then, Dove saw it – a small olive tree! She plucked off a branch and flew with it in her beak back to the ark.

"Thank God!" shouted Noah.

"Thank Raven!" cooed Dove.

"Thank Dove!" added Naamah.

This is how it all happened, way back when. And when all the animals finally left the ark, you could see two doves and two ravens, white and black, flying away together.

In the distance, God made a rainbow.

THE
BIG FISH

I was enjoying a leisurely swim in the ocean when I heard God speaking to Jonah.

"Go to Nineveh, that great city," God commanded. "Tell the people to change their evil ways."

I was sure that Jonah would listen to God, but he didn't. I had heard from the other fish how much Jonah hated Nineveh, because its people were the enemies of Israel. Jonah did not want anything to do with them.

So Jonah ran away.

Nineveh was in the east, so Jonah ran in the opposite direction. He went west.

And when Jonah had gone as far as he could on land, he boarded a ship that would take him farther and farther away.

I do not know what Jonah was thinking. Even I knew that God was not going to let him get away. God caused a great storm on the sea to get Jonah's attention. The ocean waves knocked the ship from side to side and flooded its decks.

I heard the sailors crying out. They threw some of the cargo overboard to make the ship lighter. But it did not help. I had to avoid all the boxes and supplies tumbling into the water.

Then I heard the sailors pray to their gods. But that too did not help.

Everyone was on deck trying to save the boat, but not Jonah. He was sound asleep in the bottom of the ship.

The sailors were astonished. They did not know how he could sleep through all that commotion. Neither did I.

Thunder boomed, lightning flashed, rain pounded. The ship tossed from side to side, and the angry waves crashed on the decks.

The sailors were afraid. They rowed harder. The storm got wilder. They rowed still harder. The storm got fiercer.

I dove deep into the ocean to avoid the thirty-foot waves.

Jonah said nothing, until finally, he admitted that the storm was his fault, because he had tried to run away from God. He advised the sailors, "You must throw me overboard, if you want the sea to calm down."

At first, the sailors refused.

But then they held Jonah over the side of the ship and dipped his feet into the ocean. Immediately the storm calmed. They pulled him back up again, and the waves rose against the ship. So they knew they had no other choice but to throw Jonah overboard.

As soon as they did, the sea stopped its raging.

I was just coming up for air when I opened my mouth and Jonah came gushing in.

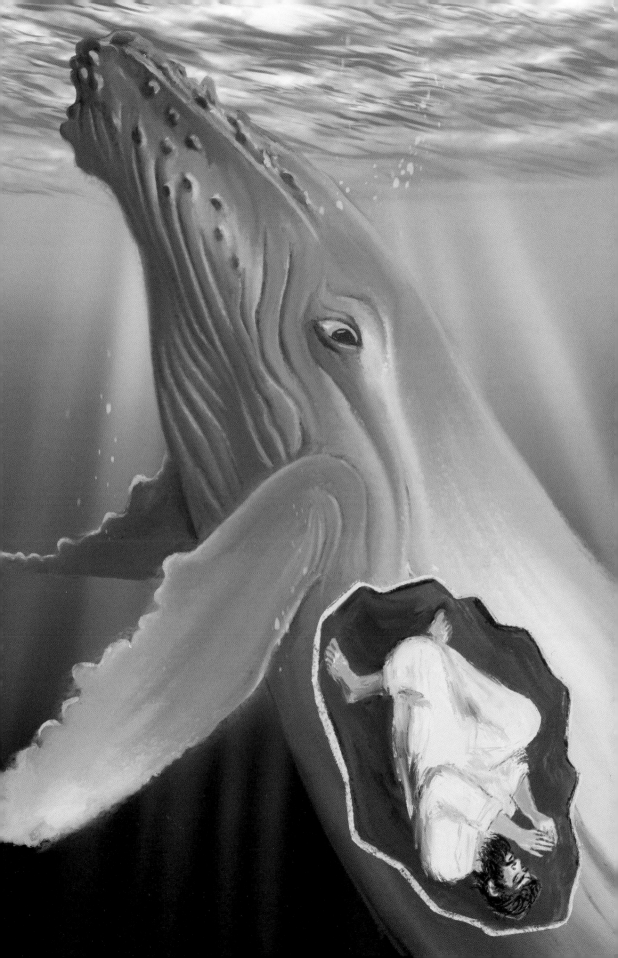

I was not at all pleased to swallow this bitter pill.

"Why me?" I asked God. "I am not more troublesome than the other fish. You know I prefer squid to humans."

There was no answer. I suppose I was just in the wrong place at the wrong time.

Without my permission, Jonah entered through my mouth, slid down my wide esophagus and landed in my belly.

The other fish had a good laugh at this sight. I had a mighty case of indigestion!

I tightened my muscles, sprayed mist out of my blowhole, arched my back, and threw my long tail in the air as I dove deep into the ocean.

I thought that this would frighten Jonah and get him to listen to God. But when I went looking for him, I found him asleep. I let out a series of squeaks that sounded like a door that needed oil. I started making clicking sounds. Still, nothing stirred in Jonah.

Finally, I shouted, "Get up, Jonah! Do you know where you are?"

He looked confused, so I told him: "You are in the belly of a big fish, my friend. And you are giving me heartburn. Just so you should know, my heart weighs about 300 pounds! Yours weighs only ten ounces!"

"Do you think I enjoy being in here?" Jonah moaned. "It is so dark and slimy." He took a deep breath and then held his nose. "Phew, it smells awful," he said.

"Is that the thanks I get for saving you from drowning?" I complained. "You don't smell so good yourself. Now, pray to God and promise you will go to Nineveh, so I can get some rest."

But Jonah refused. And then, to pass the time, he started counting my ribs and marking the days with a crab shell. It was as if he was planning to stay put. This was not going to work. So, I devised a plan.

"Jonah," I buzzed. "Get up!" Yes, he had been sleeping again. "We are going on a journey. Sit up and look through my eyes as we travel the ocean."

I could tell that Jonah was amazed that he could see through the eyes of a fish. My eyes are like glass windows, I tell you. Also, a journey sounded exciting to him. There wasn't that much to do in the belly of a big fish. With all the commotion, he had forgotten to bring something to read!

Jonah steadied himself as I began to swim and dive.

"Look to your right," I announced. "There is the path of the Sea of Reeds through which the people of Israel passed to freedom." He looked.

"Now, look on your left," I said. "There is the foundation stone of all the earth."

We traveled further. "Up in front are all the great rivers, and behind you is where the waves of the sea and its billows flow," I declared.

Then I slowed down to show him the most amazing sight of all.

"Pay close attention," I said. "These are the hills of Jerusalem and the Temple. You are standing at the Temple of God. Pray and your prayer will be answered."

I held my breath. It took a while for Jonah to say anything, but no matter, I can hold my breath for up to ninety minutes. I kept hoping that the journey had changed Jonah.

Finally, I heard him. I heard him praying:

When the waters closed over me,
When I entered the belly of the big fish,
I thought I would never see Your holy
   Temple again.
I stand in that Temple now and call out
   to You.
Listen to my prayer.
I will do what you ask!

I was overjoyed.

I sprayed mist out of my blowhole, arched my back, and threw my long tail in the air as I dove deeper into the ocean. I swam to the shores of Nineveh and then I surfaced.

There, I let Jonah go onto dry land.

I listened as God said to Jonah, "Go to Nineveh, tell the people of the wrongs they have done."

I watched from close to shore. This time Jonah did not run away.

This time I watched as he listened.

The people of Nineveh listened too. They fasted and prayed. When God saw them fasting and heard their prayers, God forgave the people and did not destroy the city.

I was pleased.

And when it was all done, I threw my tail in the air and waved as a sign of approval. But Jonah was not happy; he did not approve. Nineveh was still his enemy.

He sat all alone outside the city and frowned.

He only managed a smile when God grew a plant that shaded him from the sun. But the next day, the plant died, and he was angry again.

God was still trying to teach Jonah. Jonah was not an easy student, but I already knew that.

God asked Jonah, "If you care about the plant that grew up and died in a day, should I not care about Nineveh, that great city, with all its people?"

Jonah did not answer.

I swam away, back into the deep sea. Jonah sat alone in the hot sun.

He still had a lot to learn.

THE STUBBORN DONKEY

I am usually known as the Donkey of Balaam, as if Balaam is the important character in this story. But that is not how it really was. Let me tell you.

I had always carried Balaam wherever he wanted to go.

I never complained about going out in the hot sun, trudging up and down hills. Every once in a while, he would give me a banana as a treat.

Still, he never thanked me.

To tell the truth, I would have appreciated it if Balaam had lost a few pounds, but as I said, I did not complain.

I carried everything from large bricks, to bags of bulky vegetables, to huge stones—whatever he wanted.

I don't know why everyone makes such a fuss over horses. I am more loyal than any horse, and I need less rest, food, and water than those fancy-hooved high-steppers. The truth is, I'm an *asset*!

One time we came across a snake. Balaam was terrified.

He screamed, "Donkey, do something!"

I stared at the snake and didn't move. The snake hissed but slithered away. Sometimes it pays to be stubborn, and not let on that you are afraid.

But did Balaam thank me? Not at all.

I just took it in stride. We donkeys do that well.

Balaam had a terrible sense of direction. It didn't matter how many times he traveled to a place, he would forget which road to take, and what was worse, he would refuse to ask for directions. I was the one who steered him right when he mistakenly went left, and left when he incorrectly ventured right. I really was his comp*ass*!

Despite all I did for him, he often pointed at me and joked, "Donkey, you have goofy ears!" I guess he didn't think I had feelings.

It might have been easier if he didn't talk all the time. I often wish he would just hum a tune rather than jabber the whole journey long. Other donkeys tell me that their riders sing songs—but not Balaam.

One day he would curse, another he would bless.

He talked and talked and talked. People seemed to be afraid of his words, as if whatever he said would come true.

One day someone was making fun of him. Balaam's face turned red and he declared, "May you fall in the mud." And the man did just that—he fell facedown in the muck.

Personally, I believe that words have power, like magic. Balaam's certainly did.

I suspected trouble when the king's messengers came to talk to Balaam.

They informed him, "The king has sent us to ask you to curse his enemy, the people of Israel. He has heard that whomever you curse will fail, and whomever you bless will succeed."

I am glad Balaam did not answer right away. You had to be careful in answering a king.

"Stay the night," he told the messengers. "I will let you know in the morning."

That night, I overheard God speaking to Balaam: "Do not curse this people, because they are blessed." I was jealous. I wished God would talk to me.

The following morning Balaam sent the messengers away, saying, "Tell the king that I cannot curse this people." I knew the king would not be happy.

Next, the king sent even more messengers to plead with Balaam. "If you do as the king asks, you will be rewarded," they said.

Balaam answered, "Even if you were to give me a house full of gold and silver, I could not go against the word of God." But in the morning, something God had said, or something Balaam had dreamed, changed his mind.

Off we went.

I knew this was a bad idea.

I tried to pretend I was sick by flattening my ears, so that he would find another donkey to take him to curse Israel.

But, as usual, Balaam did not pay attention, and he just put my saddle on me and started on his journey.

After a while, we reached a very narrow path with walls on both sides. There, in front of me, was an angel, and not a very happy one. I know the difference.

People tend to imagine angels always with beautiful wings and kind faces. In other words, *angelic*. But this angel had eyes like flaming torches, and a frightening expression, and she carried a large sword.

I couldn't go back the way I came. There were walls on both sides.

And I couldn't go forward. So I turned off the path and into a field.

Balaam started yelling.

"Donkey, what are you doing?" he said.

Then, without waiting for an answer, he beat me with his staff.

This baffled me. Didn't Balaam see what I saw? He talked with God. People said he was a seer. But he couldn't see the messenger of God right before him.

With Balaam yelling, I tried to get back onto the road, but the angel was still in front of me, waving his sword.

I guess that is what it means to be between a rock and a hard place.

So I pressed close to one of the rock walls. Balaam screamed again! His foot was jammed against the wall. He pulled back on the reins with his left hand, and with his right hand he beat me again.

Well, you can't beat a dead horse, or a donkey for that matter. So, I decided to play dead and just lie down under Balaam.

It didn't seem to matter. I guess Balaam didn't care whether I was alive or dead. He just kept beating me with his staff. He was in a panic.

I twisted my head to look back at him. I wanted to tell Balaam to stop, but he never understood my donkey grunts, and I never could talk his language.

However, this time, when I opened my mouth to bray loudly, out came lots of human words. I whuffled, "What have I done to you to make you beat me?"

Balaam didn't seem as surprised as I was that I could talk his language. He only complained, "You have made a fool of me! If only I had a sword in my hand, I would kill you now."

I growled, "Am I not your donkey, which you have always ridden? Have I not carried you wherever you wanted to go? Have I ever done this to you?"

Balaam lowered his eyes a bit, and lowered that awful stick, and he said, "No, never."

I shouted, "Open your eyes! Open your eyes!"

Just then, Balaam saw the angel standing in the road with his sword drawn.

The angel opened her mouth, scolding Balaam, "Why have you beaten your donkey? If she had not turned away from me these three times, I would have killed you."

Balaam was ashamed.

"I did not see you when you were right in front of me. My donkey is wiser than I. I will do whatever you tell me," he said.

My ears perked up as I realized that God's voice could come through me, a donkey. I was going to say something but decided that was enough talking for one day.

It was then that Balaam listened to the angel, who had thankfully lowered her sword.

Only then did we travel on to see the encampments of Israelites. From then on, Balaam only spoke what the angel told him to say.

We stood above Israel in six different places and six times Balaam said words of blessing.

I guess that people make a life worthy of blessing and no amount of words can change that.

But by the time we returned home, everyone had heard about the talking donkey and the words that Balaam had spoken to the people of Israel: "How beautiful are your tents, O Jacob, your dwelling places, Israel!"

I said, "Amen!"

ILLUSTRATOR'S NOTES

A speech pathologist once helped me discover that a movie of a story or news article is more understandable to me than its written or audible version. This influences my illustration process.

First, my art director for this book and our *Pope's Cat* series, Jon Sweeney, sends me instructions for the illustrations. I read his instructions and the author's manuscript. Then I let the scene simmer in my head. After a few hours or days, it comes alive as a movie. If there's a no-show, I create the "movie." I send Jon "roughs" of the illustrations. He approves or makes suggestions.

I "watch" the movie in my head like a movie director/ editor would. I look at details which might not be in the manuscript but could help the story come alive. I gather digital images for potential "actors and props." Then I put them together and edit it endlessly for clarity and simplicity – so the viewer "gets the message" fast. I let that cook for a while. Then I come back to it and see how else I can help it read quicker and see where I can spice it up a bit. When it feels and looks good—I then sweat it out, editing and adjusting as I go—on my iPad with Procreate app.

After revisions and final approval, I exhale.

ACKNOWLEDGMENTS

To my beloved, Dennis, whose keen eye and delightful sense of humor are in these stories. And with special thanks to my publisher and friend, Jon Sweeney, who creates beautiful books. —SANDY

My gratitude to Jon Sweeney of Paraclete Press for trusting me to illustrate this book. I also thank Rabbi Sandy Sasso for trusting Jon regarding his choice of illustrator and for reintroducing me to a wonderful experience of three biblical stories about creatures of the sea, land, air, and heaven. And to life-partner Annie, who sometimes posed as a model or photographed me modeling for some of the illustrations. Finally, thanks to the Master Artist Within. —ROY

ABOUT THE AUTHOR

SANDY EISENBERG SASSO served as Rabbi of Congregation Beth-El Zedeck, Indianapolis, from 1977–2013. Dr. Sasso is presently the director of The Religion, Spirituality, and the Arts Initiative of IUPUI Arts and Humanities Institute. She is active in the arts, civic, and interfaith communities and has written and lectured on biblical storytelling, women and spirituality, and the discovery of the religious imagination in children. Sasso was ordained from the Reconstructionist Rabbinical College in 1974 and received her Doctor of Ministry from Christian Theological Seminary in 1996.

She is the author of many nationally acclaimed children's books, including *God's Paintbrush, In God's Name, But God Remembered, Noah's Wife: The Story of Naamah, God In Between, For Heaven's Sake, Butterflies Under Our Hats, The Shemah in the Mezuzah and Creation's First Light, Who Counts, The Marvelous Mustard Seed, Who Is My Neighbor,* and *A Very Big Problem* (the last four with Amy-Jill Levine). A book for adults, *Midrash: Reading the Bible with Question Marks,* has been reprinted in paperback.

Rabbi Sandy was the first woman ordained from the Reconstructionist Rabbinical College. She and her husband, Rabbi Dennis C. Sasso, are the first practicing rabbinical couple in world Jewish history. They are the parents of David (and Naomi) and Deborah (and Brad), and the grandparents of Darwin, Ari, Levi, and Raven.

ABOUT THE ILLUSTRATOR

ROY DELEON, OBLSB, is a Benedictine oblate with St. Placid Priory in Lacey, Washington, a trained spiritual director, a teacher of Blessed Movements (praying with the body, mind, heart, and soul), and of meditation.

He is the author of *Praying with the Body: Bringing the Psalms to Life*, published in 2009 by Paraclete Press.

He is also a multi-talented visual artist. As an Urban Sketcher, Roy is active on social media (Instagram @ royedeleon) showing his work.

Roy illustrated The Pope's Cat series of books, authored by Jon M. Sweeney and published by Paraclete Press. These books are favorites of Catholic children and their parents and teachers throughout the English-speaking world. The Pope's Cat series includes *The Pope's Cat, Margaret's Night in St. Peter's, Margaret's First Holy Week, Margaret and the Pope Go to Assisi*, and *Before Margaret Met the Pope: A Conclave Story*.

He lives in Bothell, Washington, with his wife, Annie.

ABOUT PARACLETE PRESS

PARACLETE PRESS is the publishing arm of the Cape Cod Benedictine community, the Community of Jesus. Presenting a full expression of Christian belief and practice, we reflect the ecumenical charism of the Community and its dedication to sacred music, the fine arts, and the written word.

Learn more about us at our website
www.paracletepress.com
or phone us toll-free at 1.800.451.5006

SCAN
TO
READ
MORE

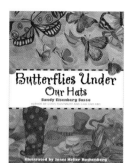